Cover Illustration by Jesus E Cordero

HOW TO HELP SOMEONE
WITH CANCER

70 Ways To Help Cancer Patients and Their Families
During Cancer Treatment

SHANNON R. BENISH

HOW TO HELP SOMEONE WITH CANCER:

70 Ways To Help Cancer Patients and Their Families
During Cancer Treatment

Copyright © 2016 by Shannon Benish

THE THINGS YOU DO FOR YOURSELF
ARE GONE WHEN YOU ARE
GONE, BUT THE THINGS
YOU DO FOR OTHERS REMAIN
AS YOUR LEGACY.

-KALU KALU

DEDICATION

To Erin & Evan, the Dynamic Duo that never left each other's side.

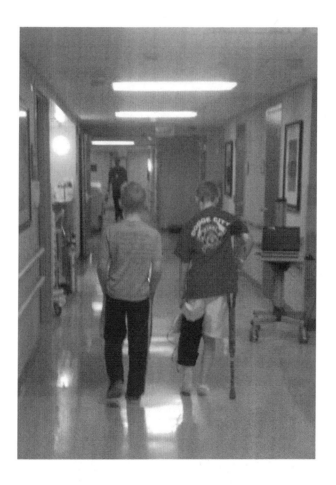

FOREWORD

My daughter Erin was only 11 years old when she was diagnosed with bone cancer. What started as a routine check-up with her pediatrician quickly turned into x-rays, scans and talk of *sarcoma*. I had never even heard of sarcoma, but from that point on we were thrust into a world in which nobody wants to belong.

We were completely blindsided and didn't know what to do. Nor did anyone else. Our friends and family offered to help but we didn't know what we needed. We struggled to maintain our normal lives, but this proved to be impossible as we had to travel six hours from home to Denver, Colorado for Erin's much needed treatments.

We were alone in a new city with a child recently diagnosed with cancer. It felt as though life was going on all around us, yet we were participating in none of it. Many days I awoke and prayed it had all just been a terrible nightmare.

Slowly we gained our footing and began the journey that became our new 'normal'. We met amazing people that have dedicated their lives to healthcare and to making a difference in other people's lives. Volunteers came and offered activities to get our minds off of the cancer and sickness. People prayed with and for us. Complete strangers wished us well. It was a challenging time, but the support we received from others carried us when it was too difficult on our own.

Oftentimes the little things people did made the biggest difference. All too often people think they can't be of help if they're unable to afford a monetary donation, but this couldn't be further from the truth! There are a myriad of ways to lend a hand that do not cost a penny but can help the patient tremendously.

This book is intended to be a guide for how to help someone who is fighting cancer or any other disease that may prevent him or her from maintaining a normal lifestyle. Although my own perspective is that of a pediatric treatment, the majority of suggestions are applicable to adult patients as well. No medical advice is given here, and I do not promote any specific treatment options. I feel that should be left to the medical professionals.

I am happy to report that Erin is now in remission and is living a happy teenager lifestyle. She loves animals, art, planning for college and anything sports related. We were so blessed to have such wonderful friends, family and community support while she was in this fight. I do not know what we would have done without them.

Never underestimate the power you have to affect someone's life for the better with a small act of kindness. No one fights alone.

INTRODUCTION

Erin had fallen on the playground the week before her regularly scheduled doctor check-up. We thought she had simply bruised her leg, but when the time came for the appointment she was still limping. We requested an x-ray be taken to ensure there had been no significant damage done in the fall. A mass was then discovered in her leg, but could not be identified without further testing.

We sought the input of a local orthopedic surgeon, and he put us in contact with Dr. Wilkins of Colorado Limb Consultants, the physician who would perform a biopsy to identify what we were dealing with. The events of those initial days are a blur as we were very much in survival mode. The trip to Denver was filled with phone calls and clouded with a surreal feeling of disbelief.

Erin was strong and courageous during the biopsy, choosing only to play a video game as a distraction during the procedure. Seeing the instruments on the table that would be used to perform the test was frightening. No child should have to be subjected to something so horrifying, yet we knew it was necessary. Some adults are not willing to choose this procedure without sedation in the hospital, yet she handled the test with the resolve of someone three times her age. The sample was taken, and we returned home to wait.

The surgeon called a couple of days later, and our worst fears were confirmed: the mass was cancerous. Family came to the house that night and we held each other and cried. Her oncologist, Dr. Clark, called that evening and introduced herself. When she spoke to Erin she told her to pack boxing gloves as she was going to beat this cancer. We loved her immediately.

We headed back to Denver to begin the hardest ten months of our lives. Surgery was scheduled to remove the tumor in her leg by performing a limb salvage procedure that would hopefully avoid amputation. The objective was to remove the cancer and insert a prosthesis where the damaged bone would be removed. I learned there is little more terrifying than watching a surgical team wheel your child away for a major surgery. We put our faith in God and prayed for the surgeons to take care of our daughter. We felt enormous relief when the doctors came out to meet with us. The surgery was a great success! But she now had a very long journey ahead.

Erin would become so violently ill during the rounds of chemo that she was unable to eat. We discussed using a feeding tube as she had lost so much weight. She struggled to keep up with school and would attend as much as possible while home, on break from her treatments, then Skype with the class and email assignments while away in Denver. We signed up for a Denver library card and utilized it as much as her health would allow. One day however, her blood cell counts were so low it was not safe to take her into the busy library around so many other people where she could risk picking up a virus or an infection. We parked outside to use the library's wi-fi as she worked from the car on a project that was due. As I look back I am utterly amazed at what she shouldered.

We tried to maintain our jobs as treatment progressed and continued working as much as possible when home. A makeshift office was built in the closet of the Denver home so I could work remotely while away. Required continuing education classes were even taken online in the infusion center while Erin was receiving chemo. You can get very creative when there is no other option!

A six hour commute after a late hospital discharge would put us home in the middle of the night so working and attending school the following day proved challenging. A saving grace would be a home-cooked meal delivered by a friend when our refrigerator was bare and there was no energy to go to the grocery store.

My mother-in-law moved in to take care of Erin's younger brother Evan while we were away in Denver. I don't know what we would have done without her. She managed everything we couldn't juggle while away and ran the household in our absence.

Evan was a huge support to Erin during her treatment and his only mission during that time was to make life better for her. I vividly remember asking him what he wanted for Christmas that year and his only wish was to have his sister home and for her to no longer have cancer. Many children would have longed for the newest video games and toys, but his only wish was for her. We were blessed with an amazing and compassionate son.

Due to our unreliable cell reception in Denver, connecting with friends and family became a struggle. My friend Amy established a Facebook page for "Team Erin". She, my friend Lynnette, and my sister Shelly became our communication support team. We were able to update our loved ones in a group when responding individually was not an option. I am so thankful for their help in keeping everyone posted when we could not, as we knew there was much concern and repeated requests for updates.

During our trips to Denver we resided at the DoubleTree Hotel for most stays at the beginning of her treatment. Some employees followed Erin's story on Facebook and always made sure we were well taken care of during our travels. On one particular trip they surprised Erin with a Colorado Rockies Build-A-Bear. To them we were more than just the next guests checking in; they took a genuine interest in us as a family. They were also there to celebrate with us after she finished treatment and when we had to return only for subsequent scans. It's not easy to live out of a hotel, but they made us feel at home there. It was so much more than good customer service; it was being there for a little girl fighting for her life. That bear meant more to her than those employees will ever know.

Though the hotel staff were wonderful, it is much easier to live in a home than a hotel. We were fortunate that part way through our treatments in Denver a generous family opened their home to us. We moved from the hotel into their house for the remainder of our relocation to Denver. We were able to begin cooking regular meals again and access a laundry machine without having to go to a public and often crowded laundromat when Erin's counts were low and the risk of infection so high. We will forever be grateful to them for their enormous act of kindness. I truly believe there are angels among us.

During treatment, one of Erin's classmates came up with the idea of a fun run as a fundraiser to help with her expenses. Countless hours of planning and organization brought together many participants that ran and walked for Erin that day. Friends and family came from miles around. Words cannot express our thanks to the Foster family and everyone that came together to make that day such a success. We were completely overwhelmed by the amount of support that was shown and humbled that so many people were behind her.

As these examples have shown, you don't have to be rich to change a person's life. Small gestures can have an enormous impact, and I'm going to show you how. YOU have the power to make a huge difference to someone right now. YOU can make what they are fighting just a little bit smaller. YOU are going to make a positive impact on someone's life.

Now let's get started and become someone's hero as they fight back!

CATEGORY INDEX

There are two ways to approach the information in this book. First, you can use the index below to go to specific categories that you wish to explore.

Second, you may read cover to cover and note the suggestions you are interested in, those that might apply to your situation. As you will see, some suggestions are included in more than one category.

Whichever your preferred method, please remember these are only starting points and there are many ways to help. Start by listening to the patient's needs and you can then formulate a plan to help.

HOW TO HELP SOMEONE WITH CANCER

1. *Make Them A Meal*

❖ This suggestion is usually one of the first things that comes to mind – and for good reason. Everyone needs to eat, and taking care of meal preparation can be of great help to a patient and their family. If you do not live in the same town as the patient don't let that stop you from helping with meals. Research restaurants in the area that deliver and have meals sent directly to their doorstep. Make sure to verify with the family the best time for delivery, and any food preferences or allergies.

If you do live nearby you can use an online meal planning service like "Take Them a Meal" www.takethemameal.com. This is basically a coordinating website where you can sign up the family, and then friends and neighbors can schedule when and what meals they will make and deliver. This allows all those who want to help to coordinate what is being made and the exact delivery schedule so there is no duplication. Short on meal ideas? There are even suggested meals that travel well right on their website, as well as recipes. Meal Train www.mealtrain.com is another planning site that can be used.

Remember to deliver the meal in disposable containers or containers you don't need back so the family doesn't have to track down the owners. Sometimes there are several people donating at one time and it is difficult to keep track of who has donated what dish.

Consider doubling your recipe and taking them an extra for the freezer. Don't forget crock pot meals as well. Several can be made ahead of time and then frozen, to be pulled out and used at a later date. If you choose this option, include thawing and cooking directions with the meal.

2. Set Up A Facebook Or Caringbridge Page

❖ As news of the diagnosis spreads among family and friends, many well wishes are conveyed and questions asked about how the patient is doing. Group updates can be a great way to communicate with friends and family to let people know how treatment is progressing. You can set up pages at www.facebook.com or www.caringbridge.org to relay updates to your whole group at one time.

Some people do not want public notification of personal matters, so privacy settings can be helpful. For example, you can create a "secret" group on Facebook and only invited members will receive status updates. It is very important to talk to the patient about their privacy wishes before sharing any information, and then respect those wishes, even if you do not agree.

As mentioned previously, Amy created a Facebook page for "Team Erin" that allowed us to post updates as we wished, and it was incredibly helpful. There were days we were so exhausted we could not contact everyone who had called or sent messages. We wanted so badly to be able to personally respond but we knew this was not an option. The ladies acted as administrators on the page so they could post updates for us when we were unable. It was such a help to us to have the means to update everyone at once.

The page was also helpful for others to share their prayers and well wishes directly with Erin. I know it gave her strength to see the number of people praying for and supporting her during treatment.

3. Help Find Lodging

❖ If travel is required for treatment, the patient will likely need lodging if they are a considerable distance from home. Costs can add up quickly and it might be hard for them to find lodging in an unfamiliar city while they are at the hospital or treatment facility.

Online websites like www.hotels.com, www.priceline.com and www.hotwire.com can be helpful when searching for lodging. Most hospitals will also be able to provide you with a list of participating hotels in the area that offer reduced rates for patients using their facility.

If a child is going through treatment, a Ronald McDonald House may be an option for the family. They are wonderful facilities that offer a "home away from home" feel. Many volunteers are responsible for these facilities and some families, church organizations and businesses even sponsor meals and activities for the families that are staying in the house. To search for locations visit: www.rmhc.org/chapter-search.

The American Cancer Society also helps to make the transition to another city easier by offering lodging through their Hope Lodge and Hotel Partners Program. Visit their website for additional information on locations and eligibility requirements.

4. Offer Computer Assistance

❖ Researching information online can be helpful. In some cases a patient may not have access to a computer (or have any inclination to use one) but wants to find out more about their condition. You can offer to help research the diagnosis, treatment options and even support groups. It is easy to forget that not everyone is tech savvy. Many people might need some help navigating through the web.

Keep in mind there is a vast amount of information online and it can be overwhelming and at times not always accurate. Make sure when researching that you are referring to reputable websites. The Children's Cancer Association has compiled a comprehensive list of resources and information for a pediatric cancer diagnosis that can be found at http://joyrx.org/resources/. You can download the resource list online or request a copy by mail.

Adult patients can refer to the American Cancer Society website at www.cancer.org. There they will find a tremendous amount of resources where a patient can research and gain additional information.

Financial resources are sometimes available through different foundations that help with the cost of cancer treatment. Some assist with travel or meal expenses, insurance co-pays or prescription medicine. Researching online can help put the patient into contact with people who may be able to help them. Searching by the specific type of cancer may be helpful as some foundations focus on a specific cause.

5. *Add Patient To Prayer List At Church*

❖ Prayers are powerful and you can never have too many. Oftentimes a patient's church family is considered extended family, and the congregation will want to lend a helping hand as well.

Do make sure to ask permission from the patient first before notifying the church in case they would rather not share the news of their health battle with the public. Some people will rather keep their health information private and that should be respected.

Did You Know?!

The number of people living beyond a cancer diagnosis reached nearly 14.5 million in 2014, and is expected to rise to almost 19 million by 2024.

To learn more visit: www.cancer.gov/about-cancer/understanding/statistics

6. *Monkey In My Chair*

❖ If a child has been diagnosed with cancer there may be fewer options for treatment as not every facility offers pediatric care. This means in many cases a child must travel away from his/her home and school during treatment. Monkey In My Chair is a great activity for younger school-age kids if they have to be away from school and their friends.

A stuffed animal monkey attends school in the place of the student when they are unable to be in class. Classmates and teachers keep the monkey involved in classroom activity and will share with the patient what the monkey does while in school. This is a great way for a child to still feel connected to their classmates and teachers. Erin's monkey not only went to class but spent time with her friends over summer break and went on some pretty amazing vacations!

To learn more about this program please visit: www.monkeyinmychair.org.

"Monkey" with Allie and Erin

"Monkey" attending school with Evan

7. Pet Care

❖ While in treatment patients will still need a plan for taking care of their loved animals. Vaccinations still need to be kept up to date and dogs will still need to be walked. It could be a win/win situation if you can get in some exercise while helping out a friend!

In some cases, with a longer treatment plan, it might be necessary for pets to stay in a foster home for a period. If you could open your home to their pet it would be reassuring for them to have their loved one with someone they trust.

8. Donate Gift Cards

❖ Donating gift cards to the family is one way to help lessen some of the patient's expenses during treatment. If you are not able to be there in person it also makes giving from a distance easier, as the cards can be mailed directly to the patient. There are many types of cards to choose from: gas cards, grocery store cards, pre-paid visa cards, phone cards and fast food restaurant cards just to name a few.

Some patients may have received their diagnosis and were rushed to a hospital in a different city with little more than the clothes on their backs. Gift cards to common stores like Target and Wal-Mart can help with getting necessities they may not have been able to pack.

For the teenager in treatment, a card for entertainment such as Amazon, Barnes & Noble, iTunes, GameStop or Xbox Live would be greatly appreciated.

One of Erin's positive memories during treatment was the day she was able to "break out" of the hospital for a short time during an extended hospital admission. She was still wheelchair-bound but we were able to go to a nearby Starbucks and she enjoyed a delicious cake pop. That donated Starbucks card gave us more than the donor will ever know. It was a chance for Erin to experience a bit of "normal" during the storm. Sometimes it really IS the little things that can mean so much. Watching her smile that day was priceless.

9. *Set Up A GoFundMe Page*

❖ www.GoFundMe.com is a crowdfunding website that enables people to go online to make donations to individuals or specific causes. Establishing a GoFundMe page allows donors to make their donation online and the funds are sent directly to the patient. When a campaign is started it can also be shared on social media and by email so you can help spread word of the fundraising effort.

The GoFundMe site also allows for updates to be posted so people can be kept up to date with any recent information that has been added to the page.

Obviously setting up a fundraising campaign like this should be approved with the patient prior to establishing the event or giving out any information. As mentioned previously, it is very important to respect the privacy wishes of the patient. Not everyone is comfortable with sharing personal information with the public or with accepting monetary donations from people they don't know well.

10. Donate Hotel Reward Points

❖ Some hotels offer the accumulation of reward points and will also let you donate them to another reward member. These reward points can then be converted to free or reduced cost rooms.

If the patient or family is staying in a hotel during treatment, expenses can add up fast. This is a way to help reduce their costs. If there is a hotel near the treatment facility, check if they have a reward program. You can also enlist the help of friends or family if they are interested in donating points.

Did You Know?!

Dogs can be diagnosed with osteosarcoma (bone cancer) just like humans. There is research being conducted at Colorado University that is helping to find treatment options for dogs and humans alike. In some cases both dogs and humans are able to use the same chemotherapy treatments!

To learn more visit: www.csuanimalcancercenter.org/

11. Take Healthy Snacks To The Hospital

❖ Access to healthy meals and snacks is not always an option during a hospital stay. Depending on when the admission occurs and on the different procedure times, the patient or family members might not always make it to the cafeteria during open hours. During long hospital admissions they might just need a break from the regular menu as well.

Most hospitals will have vending machines available, but ironically, they are not usually stocked with healthy choices. Pop and chips may get us by in a pinch but our bodies need energy long term. A visit to the hospital with some healthy snacks like nuts, peanut butter, apples, bananas or a homemade trail mix would be appreciated. (Verify the patient does not have food allergies before bringing nuts and peanut butter into their room.) If a refrigerator is available you can take items like grapes, strawberries, cottage cheese, yogurt or hard-boiled eggs.

12. *Pick Up The Phone*

❖ If you can't visit or if it's not safe due to the patient's immunity, pick up that phone and give them a call! If they can't talk, leave a message so at least they know you are thinking about them.

Patients can begin to feel very isolated during treatment. Friends and family may not visit as often because they are uncomfortable with the situation and don't know what to say, so they stay away. At the very time they need it most, the patient's support system may be shrinking.

Cancer survivor Emily McDowell said it best in her blog: "The most difficult part of my illness wasn't losing my hair, or being erroneously called "sir" by Starbucks baristas, or sickness from chemo. It was the loneliness and isolation I felt when many of my close friends and family members disappeared because they didn't know what to say, or said the absolute wrong thing without realizing it."

Your loved one needs you. Nothing has changed, yet everything has changed. They are the same person needing your friendship, enjoying your companionship and conversations, yet they have an enormous cloud surrounding their everyday life. Without the normalcy of continued friendship they can start to feel overwhelmed by the cloud.

Don't be afraid to call. Follow their lead, if they want to discuss cancer, go ahead. If they want to ignore that topic, don't mention it. The best thing you can do is to remind them you are still there, and they are never alone.

13. Help A Parent With School Activities

❖ From bake sales to carnivals, parent teacher conferences to crosswalk duty, you name it: a parent is always busy with school activities. Is there something that you can volunteer to take over for the parents?

This might be as simple as taking a shift in the carpool rotation or bringing a pie for a bake sale. It doesn't sound like much but even the pie would be tremendous help to someone unable to get to the store for supplies or without the time to spend in the kitchen.

Are you a teacher or the parent of a child who also attends the same school? If you are regularly on school grounds you can volunteer to relay notes and other information that is sent home such as permission slips, lunch ticket and milk orders and other classroom activities. If that is not an option it could be suggested to the school that notes be emailed directly to parents versus left in a child's school bag, only to be discovered weeks after the event.

14. Plant & Maintain A Garden

❖ There are many patients that love to garden but may be physically unable to do so during their treatment. During Erin's treatment she was unable to have gifts of flowers or plants due to the possibility of bacteria and infection during her time of reduced immunity.

If you could help tend their garden and allow the patient to continue to have fresh home-grown produce it would be greatly appreciated. Along those same lines, if you are a gardener yourself, think about sharing your bounty during harvest. Healthy fruits and vegetables are important to all of us but especially for a patient that needs to focus on maintaining a good diet while trying to build up strength.

15. *Treat Patient To A Day Out*

❖ Treatment can be exhausting. It can deplete your energy and leave you feeling awful. Sometimes a pamper day out can be a wonderful experience to get someone feeling better again.

Be flexible with your plans however, as they may change depending on the patient's immunity. Oftentimes large crowds may need to be avoided if there is a chance that the patient could catch a bug that their body cannot fight due to compromised immunity.

Plan a relaxing day getting a massage, shopping, visiting a favorite restaurant, going to a sporting event or just taking a short road-trip. A person can sometimes feel better just by having a change of scenery and being away from the daily reminders of the illness.

Did You Know?!

If you donate 1 pint of blood you can potentially save 3 lives?

Every two seconds someone in the U.S. needs blood.

Nearly 21 million blood components are transfused each year in the U.S.

More than 1.8 million people are expected to be diagnosed with cancer in 2016.

Many of them will need blood, sometimes daily, during their chemotherapy treatment.

To learn more visit: www.redcrossblood.org

16. *Pick Up The Patient's Mail*

❖ If the patient will be away from home for extended periods of time it may be helpful for their mail to be put on hold or picked up while they are away. If they would like it to be held by the post office they can request "Hold Mail Service" on the USPS website at: https://holdmail.usps.com/holdmail.

If this is not an option and their mail needs to be examined on a more regular basis, you can offer to pick it up and contact them if anything needs attention prior to their return.

17. Set Up A Phone Tree

❖ Not everyone is comfortable sharing personal information on social media, but it becomes increasingly difficult to contact everyone regarding each test result, travel plan, etc. that you want to update during treatment.

When a phone tree is established you can have a select group of people help to share the information you want to pass along.

It's also important to remember that not everyone is connected by social media. Great Aunt Irma might really appreciate a phone call if she wants to be kept in the loop but isn't a member of the patient's Facebook page!

18. *Offer A Ride To Treatment*

❖ Some patients do not have the means to get to treatment or feel well enough to drive themselves. If you are able to offer transportation assistance it could be of great help.

The American Cancer Society also has a program called "Road to Recovery" for patients that need assistance with transportation to treatment. To find out more about eligibility requirements of the program or to volunteer to be a driver, visit:

www.cancer.org/treatment/supportprogramsservices/road-to-recovery

19. *Make Or Send The Patient A Gift Basket*

❖ Delivering a surprise gift basket can be an immediate spirit lifter to the patient. Try to personalize the package with items that have special meaning. Do they love Grandma's chocolate chip cookies? Get the recipe and bake a special batch to include in the basket.

If the patient will be staying in the hospital, you can include items like an extra phone charger, book light or small flashlight, ear plugs, gum, ChapStick (non-petroleum based if oxygen is being used), socks with grips, eye mask, snacks and a magazine.

If you are unable to deliver something in person you can order a basket online and have it delivered. A package out of the blue is sure to bring a smile and lets the patient know they are on your mind.

A care package was delivered to the hotel while we were in Denver for treatment. When Erin realized she had mail she opened the package and was grinning from ear to ear.

You see, Erin has a special love for Bill Self, the coach of the University of Kansas basketball team. Her thoughtful teachers knew that and included many KU items in the package, as well as an autographed picture from Bill Self.

She truly felt all the love that was packed into that one box. That afternoon she forgot about being a patient and just enjoyed the moment. She read over the many cards that were sent from her classmates and teachers and felt so happy to be remembered.

I also want to mention an amazing non-profit group that

helped us in an enormous way during the initial weeks of Erin's first hospital admission. Food is one of the last things on your mind when you are bringing your child in for chemotherapy. The organization "There With Care" left surprise care packages of snacks for us in the hospital room when she was admitted. I remember thinking "How did they know?" and "What would we have done without them?" Not only do they serve the Denver area but plans are in the works for national expansion. What an amazing group of volunteers! We thank you from the bottoms of our hearts.

More information about this group can be found at: www. therewithcare.org.

"It's Bill Self!"

20. *Attend Doctor Appointments*

❖ If the patient is a close friend or family member they may appreciate you attending their doctor appointments for moral support. But ask permission first, don't just assume!

It may feel good to have a friend there, and it's nice to have a second set of ears that may catch things that one person does not. When you receive a cancer diagnosis your head is swimming with questions and fear. Yet while you are thinking about your questions, the doctor may be reviewing important information that you may miss. Having another individual ask questions and process the information can be invaluable.

Write down any questions or concerns the patient may have prior to the doctor appointment so they can be taken with you. Take notes during the visit, and in the event the patient has questions, you can review the information with them after the consultation.

Did You Know?!

Did you know that in 2014 Ronald McDonald House served over 5.7 million children and families? Not only do they provide housing to families while their child is in treatment but they also maintain volunteer rooms in select hospitals and offer scholarship opportunities for college students.

We stayed at a Ronald McDonald House during a portion of Erin's treatment and it was a wonderful experience. The staff and volunteers were so caring and always went above and beyond to create a "home away from home" feel.

Volunteer organizations, church groups and even private families provide meals and activities for the families staying in the house. It was heartwarming to see the show of support for the patients.

Ronald McDonald House relies upon many volunteers and donors to allow the facility to operate. There are numerous ways you can help support your local RMD House or RMD Room. You can donate cleaning supplies, pantry items, small unopened toys, laundry soap and fabric softener, just to name a few necessary items. Inquire at your local house for a list of items that are currently needed.

You can also volunteer your time at a local Ronald McDonald House or Ronald McDonald room at the hospital, host a meal night, provide snacks for the house, or donate tickets to local events for the families staying in the house.

Care packages can even be delivered for special occasions. One organization assembled Mother's Day bags and left them in the room for each mom. It was so touching to get back from the hospital and find that surprise waiting for us.

For more information on Ronald McDonald House visit: www.rmhc.org

21. Help With Housekeeping Chores

❖ Cancer can be physically exhausting. Trying to take care of normal household chores can be taxing to someone that already has no energy.

An easy way to help the patient is to lend a hand with housekeeping and chores they have been unable to tackle. If you can dust, clean bathrooms, vacuum, mop floors or even clean out the refrigerator you will be helping out tremendously. Did you ever think you could be a hero just for doing laundry?!

22. *Decorate Medical Aids*

❖ Unfortunately a cancer diagnosis may also mean surgery is necessary to remove the discovered tumor. A medical aid like a cane or crutch is sometimes necessary for either a short or extended amount of time during recovery.

Canes, crutches and even wheelchairs can be decorated to fit the personality of the patient. Specialty paint and even duct tape can be used to cover the aid. Although this might apply more to a pediatric patient, there are many adults that would also like to jazz up the boring "accessories". Erin inspired an amputee in the hospital who was going home to decorate his prosthesis after seeing her camouflage crutches!

Walgreens offers a nice supply of decorated canes that come in a variety of patterns and colors. Erin loves camouflage, so we modified her crutches with camouflage duct tape so she would find them a little more fun. As she progressed to using a cane it was modified to KU basketball colors. She was also given a small pouch that attached to her crutches that allowed her to carry small items like a stuffed animal or her writing utensils during school.

Treatment is not a fun time, but why not make the best of a bad situation? Any small activity you can do that makes the patient happier is worth it in my book!

23. *Winterize House And Help Outside During Inclement Weather*

❖ In some areas of the country a season change means work that needs to be done outside to prepare for the coming change in weather. There are many ways in which you can help the patient prepare their home: applying of winterizer to the lawn, disconnecting garden hoses, raking leaves, fixing drafty windows, cleaning gutters, or hiring a professional chimney sweep. Also be sure to check their supply of ice melt or sidewalk salt, and make sure they have snow shovels and ice scrapers.

When inclement weather hits you can scrape car windshields or grab a shovel and clear the driveway and sidewalks. If you are physically unable to do this yourself, are there any neighborhood kids that can be hired to help out? This may create a huge sense of relief for someone that is snowed in and needs to get out for a doctor's appointment or a treatment session.

24. Give A Gift Subscription To Netflix

❖ So much time is spent waiting during treatment, whether in waiting rooms, doctor's offices or hospital cubicles. Watching a movie can be a fun way to pass the time or get your mind off treatment for a while. Young children can have a hard time waiting for long periods, and a movie can help occupy them during an extended appointment or hospital admission.

Netflix has a mobile streaming option available that lets you watch movies on demand. For more information on purchasing a gift subscription go to www.netflix.com. There are many genres available so there is something for everyone's interests.

25. *Be A Bone Marrow Donor*

❖ If you were given the chance to save someone's life, would you? Being a bone marrow donor is one small action that might give you that power.

Every three minutes someone in the United States is diagnosed with a blood cancer. Some that have been diagnosed with leukemia, lymphoma and sickle cell anemia can be cured with a bone marrow transplant. Could you be their match?

Registering online with the Bone Marrow Registry is very easy, and after a few short health questions you can request a test kit be mailed to you. After a cheek swab is completed you mail the kit back and after testing you will be included on the registry.

A patient's likelihood of finding a donor match on the registry ranges from 66% to 97%. People between the ages of 18 and 44 are selected as a donor by physicians more than 95% of the time.

Did you know that you can also help save a life by donating the cord blood when you have a baby? More than 25,000 patients around the world have received cord blood transplants because the parents chose to donate to a cord bank.

Visit their website at: www.bethematch.org to learn more interesting facts and to find answers to many frequently asked questions.

You could be someone's cure.

Did You Know?!

Only 4% of U.S. federal funding to the National Cancer Institute is solely dedicated to childhood cancer research. Think about that for a minute: only 4%. Look at your children, grandchildren, nieces and nephews. If they were diagnosed with cancer, would 4% be enough? We must work together to raise awareness and get this inequality changed. Our children deserve more than 4%.

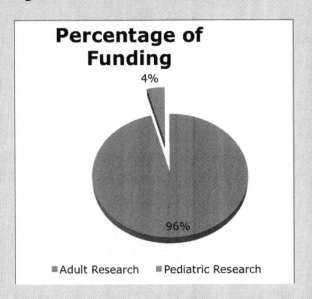

To learn more visit: www.stbaldricks.org/filling-the-funding-gap

26. Take Patient Wig & Clothes Shopping

❖ Losing their hair can be a traumatic event for cancer patients. Some people opt to shave their heads when hair first starts to fall out so they have control over when it's lost. Ordering a wig can sometimes give the feeling of control again.

Shopping for a wig can be an emotional experience and much easier with a friend. It can also feel liberating as the patient sees her appearance looking more like herself again. When the ordering of the wig is finished, think of it as a small victory against cancer and go out to celebrate. Life can feel just a little better after some rocky road ice cream or a fun movie!

If a woman has a mastectomy or lumpectomy, she may have trouble finding clothes that fit well or feel flattering. It may also be necessary to purchase new undergarments if she did not undergo reconstructive surgery. It makes a person feel good when she is comfortable in her clothes and not self-conscious about her appearance. Shopping with a friend can also be good therapy. Take time to smell the roses and enjoy spending time together outside of the hospital or treatment facility.

For those wishing to shop online a wide variety of items such as wigs, mastectomy products and headcovers can be found at www.tlcdirect.org.

27. Go Visit

❖ If the patient is up to having company (check first) then go visit if possible. Make sure you are healthy! A patient in treatment often has a compromised immune system and you do not want to expose them to anything if you are not feeling well.

Have a good time! Focus on life outside of cancer. Laugh, be silly, enjoy the friendship and just remember the patient wants to be viewed as themselves, not just as a "sick" person.

28. Donate Financial Assistance

❖ Going through cancer treatment can have an enormous financial impact on a household. To say treatment is costly would be a gross understatement. The patient not only has treatment and procedure costs, but there are many hidden costs as well. For example, if treatment requires travel you are now adding the cost of gas, lodging, parking and meals. The costs of eating on the road or even at a hospital cafeteria can add up very quickly.

Some individuals do not have insurance, and those that do will often face the reality of a procedure being denied coverage and will be forced to pay out-of-pocket. There are also co-pays to consider, and with each calendar year deductibles start over. We haven't even mentioned the high cost of medications and lab testing. The list goes on and on.

Many patients are unable to work during their or their child's treatment, resulting in lost wages. Unfortunately the mortgage or rent payments, as well as regular household bills such as utilities and car payments, do not stop during treatment. Without an adequate emergency fund even a short term job loss can be devastating.

It is hard for a patient to ask for help, but it is assured that if you are able to offer financial assistance they will greatly appreciate your generosity. The donated funds could be used to offset treatment costs, prescriptions, travel expenses, housing expenses, utility bills and even groceries.

29. Send a Card

❖ This is such a small gesture that can mean so much. We received many cards during Erin's treatment and I swear they always seemed to arrive at the best possible time. You would be amazed at how something so simple can make such a big impact, and remind someone they are not alone and are in your thoughts.

And for those times when a "get well soon" card just won't cut it for a situation so serious, check out these wonderful empathy cards by cancer survivor Emily McDowell at the Emily McDowell Studio: www.emilymcdowell.com/collections/empathy-cards. They are perfect for when you just can't find the words for such a heavy issue.

30. Send Prayers

❖ I believe in the power of prayer. We experienced many miracles during Erin's treatment and I firmly believe it was because God was watching over her. Many people asked us how they could help, and we repeatedly asked for prayers. Can you set aside a certain time in your day to say a prayer for the patient? Let them know! If you are praying for them every day at 5 pm for example, they will know they are specifically being thought of at that exact time every day.

God-wink. Noun. (plural **God-winks**) An event or personal experience, often identified as coincidence, so astonishing that it is seen as a sign of divine intervention, especially when perceived as the answer to a prayer.

One of my favorite God-winks was in the parking lot at the hospital. I had gotten out of my car and when I looked down I saw a paper that said, "She's going to make it." I don't know who it belonged to or who dropped it but I know I was meant to see it. I immediately felt more at peace during a time in which I was definitely struggling. Another God-wink was from a Panda Express fortune cookie that read, "Any troubles you may have will pass very shortly." (I know, God works in mysterious ways!)

When your child faces a life threatening situation your entire world changes. Sometimes those little God-winks come at just the right time and offer much needed reassurance that you are not alone.

Leading up to Erin's limb salvage surgery I had been a nervous wreck. The plan was to save her leg and replace the damaged bone with a prosthesis. However, we knew amputation was still a possibility if something unexpected came up during the procedure.

Surgery day came and an amazing peace fell over me. To this day I am convinced that it was due to the prayer army that was sending thoughts our way for a successful surgery. God reminded us we were not alone.

Erin's surgery was a success and with the help of a new prosthesis she was able to keep her leg and start walking again!

Did You Know?!

Did you know St. Baldrick's Foundation hosts head shaving events to raise money for children's cancer research? It got its start in the year 2000 as a challenge between businessmen. The result was 19 bald heads and $104,000 raised for research at the Children's Oncology Group.

Fast forward to 2014 and an unprecedented $27.2 million was granted to children's cancer research. In 2015 as a result of research supported by St. Balderick's, a new drug was approved by the FDA that dramatically increases the cure rate for high-risk neuroblastoma patients. It's only the third approved drug in 20 years made specifically for kids with cancer.

For more information visit: www.stbaldricks.org

31. *Give List Of Chores They Can Choose From*

❖ Many people say, "Let me know if there is anything I can do to help," but speaking from experience, it is so very hard to ask for help. People are so well meaning, but it's a humbling experience to admit that you are not able to handle everything on your own.

Give the patient a list of things that you are able to do and they may take you up on your offer. It is much easier to ask for help when specific ideas have already been offered to you. You might suggest something to them they haven't even thought about yet. This can also eliminate duplication if something you are offering is already being taken care of by someone else in their support system.

32. *Winterize Car & Take For Regular Maintenance*

❖ Vehicles need regular maintenance to ensure optimal performance, but keeping up with regular oil changes may be the last thing on a patient's mind. Depending on location, there may also be a need for additional maintenance on a vehicle if a season change is coming. It would be considerate to help transport their vehicle to the service station as needed.

This becomes especially important if the patient is utilizing a treatment facility that is out of town. Traveling long distances will add many miles to the odometer, which in turn will require more frequent oil changes and tire replacements for the car.

33. *Offer To Take Or Make Phone Calls If Patient Needs A Rest*

❖ Sometimes communicating can be very tiring when you are telling the same story over and over again. Couple that with long days, nausea and no sleep and you will understand why the patient may not feel up to visiting. Offer to answer the phone for a while or return calls they may not have been able to make yet to allow the patient to rest.

34. Be Patient's Homework Or Workplace Liaison

❖ If a child is unable to attend school during certain periods of treatment it can be a challenge for them to keep up with homework during the absence. But if they are able to work on their studies while away, there is a good chance they will maintain the same grade level as their classmates. Some hospitals offer tutors to help the children keep up with their classmates. If possible, homework assignments could be picked up after completion and the work delivered back to the school.

Likewise, if the patient is an adult and away from their job, working from home or the hospital, they might need some help getting their work delivered back to the office. If you or a co-worker could be the contact person for returning completed work you could help them tremendously.

35. Be Patient's Schedule Coordinator

❖ Making doctor and testing appointments can sometimes feel like an uphill battle when trying to coordinate many offices at once. At one point a follow-up trip to Denver consisted of seeing Erin's oncologist, orthopedic surgeon, plastic surgeon, nephrologist and infectious disease doctor. At the hospital, CT and bone scans were conducted. Then at another location, echo, EKG & hearing tests were administered. If one person or testing time was unavailable it would throw the entire schedule out of whack. We were beyond blessed that the professional offices and hospital were located so close together.

Don't forget to make hotel reservations; nobody wants to sleep in the car. Call the school, let them know of a child's absence and arrange homework to be picked up. There is a lot to juggle. You may be able to lend a hand just by coordinating the schedule and keeping track of doctor appointments, labs and treatment sessions. The old fashioned calendar still works perfectly, or if you are more tech savvy, there are apps that you can download to track doctor and other scheduled appointments.

Did You Know?!

Did you know that dogs can be trained to be hospital volunteers?

Some hospitals have volunteers that bring their dogs to visit patients. Do you have a dog that loves people and is well-behaved? Check with your local hospital for participation in this program and their specific qualifications. You, as well as your dog, will go through specialized training before becoming a volunteer.

Erin loved when the dogs came to visit and immediately perked up when she saw them enter the room. The visits also gave her something to look forward to during long hospital admissions when she knew they were coming back. Those brief interactions always brought a smile, even on the hardest of days!

Erin with her favorite volunteers

36. Donate Blood

❖ There is always a need for blood donations. Approximately 36,000 units of blood are needed every day in the United States. Many of these transfusions are for cancer patients going through chemotherapy treatment.

Donating blood has never been easier thanks to the convenience of online scheduling and a mobile app from the Red Cross. You now even have the capability to track where your blood has been sent after the donation!

To search for a blood drive in your area visit the Red Cross website at www.redcrossblood.org/. You can also learn about the blood donation process, schedule a donation, learn about hosting a blood drive and about volunteer opportunities that are available.

Erin was in need of a transfusion multiple times during treatment. If that blood had not been available to her, we would have been in a very dangerous position. I am so thankful for the donors who took the time to give such a precious gift.

37. Run Errands

❖ It's amazing how the simple task of running errands can help someone that is not feeling well. A trip to the grocery store, post office or shopping mall might not seem like much to a healthy individual, but to someone going through chemotherapy it can be physically exhausting.

If you are heading to the grocery store make a quick call to see if there is anything you can pick up for the patient. This small gesture can mean the world to someone that can't get out easily. And running errands does not have to be limited to the grocery store, but could include anything from going to pay bills, wash the car, pick up prescriptions or even dry cleaning.

Some patients may have recently had surgery and are unable to drive themselves due to restrictions. Driving the patient to the beauty shop, doctor appointments or even to church can be a blessing to someone who is unable to do so themselves.

38. Shave Your Head In Support

❖ Losing your hair can be a very traumatic experience. When someone else is flaunting a shaved head with you it can be a little easier to bear.

Erin had many friends, classmates and relatives who shaved their heads to show support. It was a great display of solidarity and a reminder to her that she was not alone in this fight.

This could also be implemented as a fundraising event for a patient if there is a large group wanting to come together to shave their heads in support.

39. Donate Frequent Flyer Miles

❖ If traveling to another city for treatment is a necessity, the cost of travel, especially by air, can add up quickly. If you are a frequent traveler that has accumulated many miles, consider donating them to the patient or to family members that might need to accompany them during travel.

Check with your specific airline's customer service department to confirm program guidelines and to verify if this type of transfer can be accommodated.

40. Get Them A Funny Book

❖ Laughter really is the best medicine. In the midst of such a life-threatening situation it does a body good to let go and laugh for a while. Forgetting your cares and having a good chuckle is sometimes just what the doctor ordered.

Did You Know?!

Pediatric cancer isn't that rare. 1 in 285 children in the U.S. will be diagnosed with cancer before the age of 20.

The causes of most childhood cancers are unknown and are not strongly linked to lifestyle or environment, unlike many adult cancers.

Research funding has never been more important. Overall, more than 80% of children and adolescents diagnosed with cancer will live at least 5 years after their diagnosis. Let's make it more.

To learn more visit: www.thenccs.org/cancer-facts

41. Give A Gift Magazine Subscription

❖ There are countless hours to fill in waiting and hospital rooms. It is not always easy to concentrate on a lengthy novel; however, just flipping through the pages of a magazine about a favorite hobby or interest can help pass the time.

Visit with the patient about their particular interests and pick up a magazine for them to take to the doctor's office or hospital. If you wish to purchase a gift subscription there are subscription postcards within the magazine itself. You can also go online to the magazine's website or visit an online subscription service such as www.magazines.com.

42. Help Children With Homework

❖ If the parent is the patient they may have a hard time concentrating when helping their children with homework. "Chemo brain" is very real and many people have difficulty with focus and memory issues during treatment. The patient can have a hard time remembering and concentration can be a struggle. This can be an area where you could lend assistance. Don't be discouraged if the child needs help in a subject in which you are unfamiliar. There are a host of online learning sites which you can use to help tutor.

If a child is the patient, the parents are likely busy trying to help them keep up with their classes so they can advance with their classmates to the next grade. This can be especially challenging if they have missed many school days. A good resource to consult is the child's resource officer at the hospital. These individuals have a wide array of knowledge and are there to help the children and their families, so don't forget to reach out to them for ideas as well. Some hospitals have teachers on staff for children with long admissions, and others have retired teachers in the area that donate their time to tutor.

A sibling might be the one who needs additional help if Mom or Dad is busy helping a pediatric patient. If you are unable to tutor them yourself, maybe a teacher can help, and you can assist transporting the child back and forth to study sessions.

43. *Find Support Groups*

❖ When going through this type of experience, even the patient's closest loved ones may not fully understand what they are going through. They may need a connection with others who are currently in treatment or have been through it in the past for a source of suggestions or moral support.

Support groups for cancer patients may be found locally, or if not available, an internet search can yield many opportunities to connect with others online. I found an amazing group on Facebook that focuses specifically on osteosarcoma: Osteosarcoma (Bone Cancer) Survivors, Family and Friends. They are incredibly supportive and understand many of the same issues specific to bone cancer that we were dealing with. Even though Erin has completed treatment, they continue to be a wealth of information for issues that continue into remission. Support groups are not only helpful to the patient but can be a great resource to friends, family and caregivers as well.

The American Cancer Society has a search engine for support groups/resources in your area. You can search by zip code or address at:

www.cancer.org/treatment/supportprogramsservices/index?ssSourceSiteId=null

The Association of Online Cancer Resources (ACOR) is an online community for parents, caregivers, family members, and friends to discuss clinical and nonclinical issues and advances pertaining to all forms of a specific disease. For more information visit their website at: www.acor.org/.

44. Organize A Fundraiser

❖ As mentioned earlier, the expenses related to treatment are not limited to just medical expenses and hidden expenses can add up very quickly. Spread the word and you will be amazed at the number of friends and family members that want to lend a hand with fundraising efforts.

The following are some fundraising ideas that could be used to help reduce some expenses: a fun run/walk, bake sale, raffle, baseball/softball tournament, auction, garage sale, car wash, t-shirt sale, street dance, mud volleyball tournament, bracelets sale, or a battle of the bands music competition. The ideas are virtually endless, so don't be afraid to use your imagination and get creative.

Fundraiser Insight has compiled a comprehensive list of fundraising ideas that can help you think outside the box when trying to narrow down your choices. The list can be found at www.fundraiserinsight.org/ideas/. Depending on the financial need, you may find that more than one fundraiser may be necessary to help lessen the financial hardship to the family.

45. Decorate For The Holidays

❖ Nothing can brighten the spirit more than beautiful decorations for the holidays. Unfortunately the patient may not feel like putting up decorations themselves, nor have the energy to do so.

Can you lend a hand to help hang some lights or string some garland? This could even be a fun collaborative effort by a few neighbors. Then celebrate completion with cookies and hot cocoa!

This activity can help make their living space a comfortable and festive area in which to enjoy the holiday season. Make sure to consult with the patient and their doctor before using a live Christmas tree due to allergy or infection.

Did You Know?!

Vanna White, celebrity co-host of Wheel of Fortune has her own line of yarn named Vanna's Choice. Vanna donates half of all proceeds to St. Jude Children's Research Hospital. St. Jude is a children's hospital that not only treats children but continues research to find cures for cancer and other diseases.

To date, Vanna has donated over $1.7 million to the hospital.

For more information visit: www.stjude.org/about-st-jude/stories/promise-magazine/summer-2016/perspective-vannas-choice.html

46. Care For Landscape

❖ The lawn keeps growing, and a landscape will need constant care while the patient is in treatment. Lend a hand if possible or offer to hire someone if you are not in the position to physically help maintain it yourself.

There are many jobs besides the mowing that will need tending to while treatment progresses. Trees and shrubs need trimming, plants need watered, sidewalks need edged, weeds need pulled and lawn fertilizer needs applied. This is a lot of work for one individual, so don't be afraid to enlist additional help if necessary.

47. Give A Gift Membership To AAA

❖ Some people will not be able to receive treatment close to home and will need to travel to receive care. Being on the road and having AAA coverage is good peace of mind should anything go wrong with their vehicle.

A membership to AAA will also allow the patient to receive discounts at some hotels and retailers during their travel.

You can purchase a gift membership from the AAA website at: www.AAA.com or by calling 1-800-JOIN-AAA.

48. *Help With Organization Of Legal And Financial Matters*

❖ Oftentimes when someone becomes ill it is a catalyst for getting tasks completed that may have been neglected prior to the diagnosis. Getting legal matters organized is one such task. The patient may now feel like it is the time to get those items completed. Consult a trusted attorney to help with these matters; do not try this yourself.

Each situation is different and the attorney will be able to advise based on the patient's particular needs. Does the patient have an updated will? Has a trust been drawn up and funded? Has the patient granted power of attorney for legal and health matters to a trusted friend or family member? These are just a few questions to review with the attorney.

Another such task that may have been postponed is getting financial matters organized. The patient may want to meet with his or her banker, insurance agent and financial advisor to ensure accounts have been structured as intended. Financial accounts need to be titled correctly, beneficiaries need to be kept up to date, and payments should be organized to meet debt obligations.

Often there is only one individual in the household that is responsible for the finances. When that person falls ill it may be hard to decipher the account statements, bills or investment reports that may show up in the mailbox or by email. Consider setting up accounts on auto-pay so that an invoice is not missed, and take advantage of mobile banking options if available.

If the patient wants you to handle making any changes make sure they have a financial Power of Attorney (POA) as financial institutions will not act on your instructions without proper legal forms documenting your authority.

49. Connect Across The Miles

❖ With advancements in technology, keeping in touch across the miles has never been easier. You can take advantage of Skype, Hangouts, Snapchat or Facetime just to name a few possibilities.

Seeing each other "in-person" can reassure the patient that you are still there for them even if you cannot be there physically. Keeping in contact with a spouse or children that are at a distance also helps maintain a healthy relationship.

50. *Introduce The Patient To A Fellow Fighter*

❖ If you can put the patient into contact with someone who has been through cancer treatment themselves, there is a good chance that the survivor will be able to lend support and give helpful advice. When someone has "been there, done that" they have first-hand experience with the physical and emotional side-effects caused by treatment. They can likely sympathize with what the patient is feeling and offer emotional support in ways a non-patient cannot provide.

A person that has been through treatment is also likely to offer tips or advice that might make it easier for the patient to manage. For example, when Erin was in the hospital we discovered that if they administered her chemotherapy at night she slept and didn't experience the violent nausea she had become accustomed to with each round.

Mouth sores can become a patient's worst nightmare. As a preventative, a not-so pleasant tasting mouth lozenge is dissolved on the tongue. Erin realized that if she sucked on a jellybean with the lozenge the flavor was much more tolerable.

It's also worth mentioning to be mindful when using perfume, colognes and lotions with strong scents around the patient. If nausea is an issue, the strong aroma can be overwhelming to the senses and make them more nauseated.

What works for one patient will not always work for another, but those adjustments to small details made a huge difference to her! Of course it's always important to consult the doctor with any questions regarding specific treatment procedures.

Did You Know?!

Did you know that a recent study of a 1.7 million-year-old bone has concluded that the fossil shows signs of cancer? This bone was originally discovered in South Africa near the city of Johannesburg over 50 years ago.

It has been speculated that cancer has always been with us, that cancer is not only due to contributing factors like pollution and carcinogens in our diets of today. The discovery of the bone tumor lends credible evidence to the fact that cancer dates back to our early human relatives.

For more information visit the Wits University website at:

https://www.wits.ac.za/news/latest-news/research-news/2016/2016-07/hominin-cancer/

51. *Take Garbage Cans To Curb On Trash Day*

❖ It doesn't sound like much, but helping move trash cans to the curb on garbage day is enormous help to someone that may not physically be able to themselves.

As mentioned previously, surgery will sometimes be required when there is a cancer diagnosis. If a patient has recently had an operation, there is a good chance they have weight restrictions on what they are allowed to lift safely. You may be of assistance by moving items for them that they are not able to physically handle alone.

52. Offer Help As Paperwork Coordinator

❖ A small forest is cut down with each hospital admission or follow-up scan trip. This may be an exaggeration, but not by as much as you might think. There are consent-to-treat forms, privacy practice notices, financial forms, notice of patient rights and responsibilities, and forms for each specific office you visit.

Just when you feel you have climbed the paper mountain and are in the clear, you check the mailbox and there is a stack of Explanation of Benefit (EOB) forms that need matched up with billing forms. Throw in the occasional insurance letter requesting additional information – or a denial notice – and it's enough to make you pull your hair out. If you are a highly organized person you could be worth your weight in gold to a patient needing help coordinating all of the paperwork. It is also worth mentioning to keep those records for tax time. Some patients will need to have documentation of expenses to submit to their accountant for tax preparation.

In the event the patient is applying for financial assistance, they will likely be required to complete documentation forms prior to being considered for aid. If this is the case you can also offer assistance completing applications for them.

53. Donate Your Hair

❖ What a wonderful show of support to donate your own hair to an organization that will make a wig for a cancer patient! Two such organizations are Wigs for Kids and Pantene Beautiful Lengths.

PLEASE do your homework before donating! This includes both monetary or hair donations. Some organizations will charge patients for the wigs so if this is not your intention make sure your organization donates the wigs to its recipients free of charge.

Also keep in mind that each company will have their own requirements as to what color and length of hair they can accept. Verify what is acceptable BEFORE you have your hair cut as many places have very specific requirements. Most organizations have a website that gives you instructions, as well the address to where you should submit your donation.

Erin's amazing oncology doctor grows her hair out and selects one of her pediatric patients to cut it for donation each time its long enough. Erin had the honor of cutting Dr. Clark's hair one year and she could not have been more proud!

Erin cutting Dr. Clark's hair for donation

54. Help Keep Normalcy For Children

❖ Try to keep life as normal as possible by keeping some of the same routines and traditions as before diagnosis. Do you normally get donuts on the first day of school? Visit a snow-cone shop during summer? Make it a priority to maintain the activities if possible so the children will feel comfort in the regularity.

Many summer camps have been organized for pediatric cancer patients or for children of adult cancer patients. Being able to keep normalcy and engage with other children their own age and in similar situations can help tremendously.

One such camp for pediatric patients is the Roundup River Ranch. They do an amazing job of letting the kids be kids again, not focusing on cancer and limitations, but on what the kids can do. To find out more about this amazing camp visit: www.roundupriverranch.org.

It can be very hard for children, whether they or their parent or loved one are the patient, to understand cancer and what that means. It's difficult for them to understand why they or their parent is so sick and what's happening to them.

Keeping the line of communication open is very important. Fear of the unknown can be crippling to a child and open communication can help lessen their worries.

The American Cancer Society has information available that will help you talk to your child about the cancer diagnosis affecting your family. You can access the information at: www. cancer.org/acs/groups/cid/documents/webcontent/002605-pdf.pdf

55. Work On Celebration Of Life List

❖ I hesitate to call it a "bucket list" because we are here to focus on living and finding joy in the middle of the storm. So for today we will refer to our "to-do list" as a Celebration of Life list.

We have all heard the saying that "life is too short." Well my friends, it really is. When you have a loved one that has been diagnosed with a life-threatening illness your entire world and outlook changes. Things that seemed to matter before fall to the wayside and you begin to re-prioritize.

Has your loved one expressed interest in activities they wish they had done or trips they should have taken? Could you help fulfill some of the items on their list? Take a trip, a cooking class, study a second language, learn to paint, ride a horse? The sky is the limit and it may spark a renewed sense of living to get out there and try new things.

Spending quality time with your friends and family becomes more of a focus. You value people more and "things" less. Use this time to reconnect and focus on activities that make the patient happy and fulfilling wishes they would like to pursue.

Did You Know?!

Did you know there is an organization called BraveHoods that donates free t-shirt hoodies to pediatric cancer patients? For every hoodie they sell, one is given absolutely free of charge to a child that is fighting cancer. Not only do they support the cancer patient themselves, but also their siblings who might oftentimes be overlooked.

The inspiration for BraveHoods came from a 5-year-old girl named Meredith who was battling cancer and had a hard time wearing wigs, scarves and hats when she lost her hair. Her parents found that a hoodie t-shirt was the most comfortable for her to wear and let her feel like a "normal kid."

After treatment was over and having the awareness that so many children were still being diagnosed daily, Meredith's mother, Allison Yacht, and her family set out to help. Knowing the uncomfortable position that Meredith endured compelled them to find a solution – and BraveHoods was born!

If you would like to support the organization but don't need a shirt, you can also participate in the "No Shirt For You." You pass on receiving a shirt yourself and BraveHoods will send out a hoodie to two cancer patients instead!

Erin's favorite hoodie had the quote, "Veni, Vidi, Vici" on the front, which means "I Came, I Saw, I Conquered." Absolutely right, these kids are warriors.

My other favorite hoodie reads, "It's All Good in My Brave Hood." Love it!

For more information visit: www.bravehoods.org

56. Lend A Hand With The Children

❖ The world keeps turning during treatment, and so do the needs of the entire family. Children still need special attention when their parent is sick and so do other siblings if a child is the one that is ill.

During pediatric treatment, Mom and Dad often have to focus so much time and energy on the child that is sick they are unable to do things like take the other siblings to the park or on play dates.

Is there an activity you can offer to do with the children? Sporting events, concerts, a short road trip, or even just out to a movie would be a treat. Plenty of fun can be had by staying home and doing something simple like playing a board game. Planning an activity does not have to be anything extravagant. Chances are the children will just appreciate the one-on-one time and being the center of attention.

When Erin was ill we were so thankful for everyone who showed special attention to her younger brother Evan while we were away. His entire world was turned upside down and he never wanted to be away from her side. He was so supportive during treatment and his main focus was always on how he could make it better for her. I was always so touched when people would show their concern for him as well.

Babysitting can also give Mom & Dad a break to have much needed alone time.

Going through cancer treatment, whether it be adult or pediatric, can be very hard on a marriage, and being able to spend time as husband and wife, not just medical caregivers, can go a long way towards maintaining a healthy relationship. Having a date night out without focusing on cancer can be a much needed break.

57. Capture Moments The Patient Cannot Attend

❖ It's impossible to be in two places at once, and the patient will undoubtedly miss events they would love to attend. A child's school program or ballgame, wedding, anniversary, graduation, work promotion, birthday party or birth of a baby are just a few examples. Life happens all around us, even during cancer treatment.

Sometimes an absence is due to travel, sickness or a treatment session and cannot be avoided. Whatever the reason, there are many opportunities to capture special events by pictures or video and share with the patient. Sharing those missed moments will allow them to feel more included and less isolated from their own life due to the demands of treatment itself.

When out of town for Erin's treatment, our friends and family would forward pictures of Evan's school activities or other events. Seeing pictures of him made us feel more connected with the rest of our family and "normal" life.

58. Assemble A Road Trip Busy Kit

❖ If travel is involved for treatment there may be many hours spent confined in a vehicle on the road. If the family is traveling with small children it can be a challenge to keep them entertained in the car for long periods of time.

Put together a travel bag that can help keep the kids busy and pass the time more easily. It doesn't have to cost much and can be assembled with many fun items from a store like Dollar Tree. Crayons, coloring books, cards, snacks and games that the kids can play in the car are just a few ideas. There are many magnetic travel games out now such as hangman, tic-tac-toe and checkers. Don't forget a simple blank notebook and pencil for doodling and games like license plate bingo and I Spy.

A small package of tissues and baby wipes can also be useful in the kit.

59. Support Cancer Research

❖ Some patients may say they do not want any specific assistance. Rather, they just want to help put an end to this disease. Not everyone will accept help and that's OK: this is a time to respect the patient's wishes and not push.

You can donate to reputable research programs in their honor, but PLEASE do your homework prior to making any donations. You want to ensure the majority of your donation goes directly to funding the research itself.

Information can be found on a foundation's website that will itemize how donated funds are allocated.

60. Hang Out At Happy Hour

❖ Your loved one might not have the energy to get together for a long period of time, but can you take them to enjoy a quick soda or coffee at happy hour? Just sitting together for a short period and visiting about life outside of treatment can be very uplifting to the spirit.

Did You Know?!

Did you know there was an extraordinary young man named Zach Sobiech who changed the future of cancer research? Zach was diagnosed with a rare form of bone cancer called osteosarcoma. Since there are only approximately 400 pediatric cases diagnosed in the United States per year there is not a large amount of funding solely dedicated to research in that area. Zach effectively changed that!

Sobiech recorded the hit song "Clouds" and it became an internet sensation. He requested the proceeds from the sale of the song be dedicated to the Zach Sobiech Osteosarcoma Research Fund.

Sadly, Zach passed away from the disease when he was only 18 years old. His best friend Mitch Kluesner is now carrying on the vision that started with Zach. Mitch is working with the University of Minnesota to find a cure for the disease that took the life of his friend.

Due to the Sobiech funding a new therapy has been developed that uses the patient's own immune system to attack the osteosarcoma cells. Normally getting to a clinical trial can take upwards of ten years, but the trial for this new therapy is set to begin this year. Without the research funds from Zach's Foundation this would not have been possible.

I never had the pleasure of meeting Zach personally, but I think of him often. I think about how he is changing this fight and how he has provided research funds directly to the people who have really made a difference. I wish to thank him for what he has done to help find the cure for cancer. He leaves behind a legacy that is truly inspirational and has made a difference in the lives of others.

PLEASE consider downloading this song to help Zach continue his mission to find the cure! For only $ .99 YOU can make a difference.

To learn more or to download Zach's music including the hit song "Clouds" visit: www.childrenscancer.org/zach

61. Decorate Hospital Room

❖ Long hospital admissions can be depressing to say the least. Some pediatric patients can have a treatment plan that calls for month-long hospital admissions. When a patient has to be away from home for such long periods of time, making his or her hospital environment as comfortable as possible can help immensely. Decorating the room with inspiring messages, favorite toys if the patient is a child, and reminders from home can make the stay a little more pleasant.

One young patient in the room across from Erin even brought in his own microwave. Genius! No more zombie trips down the hallway to heat coffee at 3 am.

Erin's aunt gave her a pair of boxing gloves to keep at the hospital as a reminder that she was going to beat that cancer. It was a strong visual reminder of the goal at hand.

There are many products available that allow you to hang posters and decorations without doing any damage to the walls. There are also a wide variety of inspirational wall clings that can be put up and removed with ease.

62. *Pick Up The Newspaper*

❖ If your friend or neighbor is gone for extended times during treatment you can pick up their newspaper as a courtesy. Not only is it convenient for them, but it could also prevent strangers from seeing newspapers pile up in the driveway and making their home an easy target for break-ins or vandalism.

It is sometimes necessary for patients to temporarily relocate to another city and change their mailing address to their new "home away from home." Some newspapers will mail the paper out of town to its subscribers via the US Post Office. Check with the circulation department at the newspaper to see if this is an option available with their subscription. Receiving news from home might also make them feel more connected while they are away.

63. *Take A Shift At The Hospital*

❖ Not everyone is able to stay with their child or loved one while they are in the hospital. The demands of work, school or other commitments make it impossible to be in two places at once. Offer to take a shift at the hospital to keep the patient company while the other family members get a break.

If they don't want to leave the hospital, offer to bring in a meal if allowed or stay with the patient so that the caregiver can take a trip to the cafeteria or lounge area. Allowing the caregiver a break to stretch their legs and take a short walk can be restorative to their health as well.

64. Offer Care For The Entire Family

❖ A cancer diagnosis affects the entire household. Do you notice someone else in the family that might be struggling and need a helping hand? Sometimes the best way you can help a patient is to help the ones they love but are unable to assist themselves.

Unfortunately some patients are also in the role as a caregiver during their own treatment. Caring for an aging parent during cancer treatment can be especially challenging when battling their own health issues. Offer assistance as the caregiver needs. This could be taking the parent to doctor appointments, running errands, housekeeping or just spending some quality time together.

65. *Help With College Applications And Scholarship Searches*

❖ Some cancer patients may be simultaneously going through cancer treatment while also trying to further their education by attending college. On top of the mountain of medical paperwork they are battling, they will also need to complete college applications, financial aid and scholarship applications.

We have already discussed the high costs of treatment. Now couple that with the enormous cost to attend college and the result can be the patient dropping out of school as the costs are just too prohibitive.

There are organizations that recognize the struggle to pay for higher education while keeping up with medical bills or transitioning after treatment and will offer scholarships to cancer patients and survivors.

The National Children's Cancer Society offers the Beyond the Cure Ambassador Scholarship Program which awards 40 scholarships annually to childhood cancer survivors. More information can be found at www.thenccs.org/scholarship.

The Samfund has an amazing website with a wealth of information for young adult cancer survivors. There are currently over 20 links to different websites that may offer scholarship opportunities for cancer survivors and current patients. To find out more visit: www.thesamfund.org/get-help/resources/undergraduate-tuition-assistance/.

Did You Know?!

Did you know that Samfund is the first and largest nonprofit organization in the country that provides financial assistance and online support to young adults that have battled cancer?

Since 2005 they have awarded over $1.6 million in grants, and they offer a webinar series, "Moving Forward With Your Financial Health," to assist young adults in moving on with their lives after cancer.

For more information visit: www.thesamfund.org/

66. Help Monitor Medications

❖ Patients might be taking a large number of medications at one time. You can help monitor the schedule in which the medications need to be administered and the correct dosages. This can be done by using a simple pill box with days and times specified on the container, written scheduling on a notebook pad or a system as advanced as using a downloaded app that helps you track the information. A few examples are CareZone, AARP Rx and MyPillBox.

Keeping a complete list of current medication and dosages can also be very helpful in the event of an unexpected ER trip or hospital admission.

Erin's chemo treatment required a "rescue drug" and fluids that needed to be administered at very specific times throughout the day. This can become a very overwhelming process when trying to keep track of all dosages and timing, so even alarms set on a cell phone can be a helpful reminder.

67. Organize A Treatment Binder

❖ The amount of information a patient will receive from the doctor, hospital and laboratory can be overwhelming. Organizing this information in a binder can be very helpful to the patient.

Erin's oncologist provided us with a binder to collect paperwork that was also full of useful information, from what to expect during treatment, questions to ask, patient care and even future doctor appointments.

When you are keeping track of blood cell counts, numerous chemotherapy drugs, prescription medicines and dosages, medical equipment care, etc. it is very easy to forget important information. When it is kept in the same place and organized, patients can find what they need with relative ease.

If you are interested in a planner that has already been organized for you, the non-profit organization Cancer 101 has compiled a binder with this type of information already included. The binder can be found at: www.cancer101.org/toolkit/order-planner/.

68. *Donate Laptops or DVDs*

❖ Do you have a laptop or tablet sitting around that you no longer use? This can be donated to a patient that spends a lot of time at the hospital, or it can be donated to the hospital directly.

Children often have very long hospital admissions during treatment. Having access to a laptop to do homework and play games can help them pass the time.

When Erin had week-long hospital admissions we would look for different activities for entertainment. Movies would sometimes be a good distraction when she was not feeling well or taking a break from doing homework.

The resource center on the pediatric floor had a library of DVDs that were available for check-out by the children. If you have movies that you no longer watch, they can be offered to the patient, or you can contact your local hospital to see if they could be of use at the facility.

69. *Donate Sporting Event Tickets*

❖ Are you a season ticket holder that can't always make it to the game? Consider sharing your tickets with someone that might not get the opportunity to go otherwise.

When we were staying at the Ronald McDonald House someone had donated playoff tickets to a NFL game. A drawing for the tickets was held and sheer joy is the only way to describe Erin's face when she was told she had won.

To the person that donated the tickets that day, I cannot thank you enough for giving her something so special. She was released from the hospital on game day and made it to the game that very night. A new Denver Bronco fan was born!

70. *Continue Support After Treatment*

❖ Do not assume that life will return to normal for the patient as soon as the last round of treatment is completed. The patient will likely have continuing doctor visits, labs, scans and medication.

They will continue to be monitored to make sure the cancer has not returned, and with those scans comes the anxiety that a relapse is possible. The term"scanxiety" is very real and some patients may even exhibit symptoms of a form of post-traumatic stress disorder (PTSD). The patient has experienced a traumatic experience and the transition to returning to "normal" life can be an adjustment. Be supportive and let them know you are still there. Just listening to their concerns can be extremely reassuring to them.

To learn more about how PTSD affects cancer survivors visit: www.curetoday.com/publications/cure/2014/summer2014/ post-traumatic-stress-disorder-after-cancer

For valuable information on transitioning back into life after cancer visit: www.cancer101.org/i-am-a-survivor/

Last day of treatment!

CONCLUSION

Cancer is a thief, and it steals so much: power, faith, freedom, innocence, peace or even life. Our hope for the future is that this book will no longer be needed, and we will have found a cure for this dreadful disease.

It is important to support your loved one in any way possible as they are in the fight of their life. Focus on the positive. There is always something to be thankful for. Celebrate life and keep a positive outlook. Be a good listener and have regular conversations that don't revolve around cancer.

Don't make decisions for the patient unless asked, and don't talk around them as if they weren't in the room. Don't judge. This battle is not yours and not everyone makes the same decisions. What's right for one person may not be acceptable for another, and one size doesn't fit all.

Refrain from recommending alternative treatments; leave that up to the professionals. Don't ask the patient how they "got" the cancer. The majority of people will never know and they don't need to second guess themselves. This is not the time to focus on the past, only the present and fighting this enemy.

Show compassion and understanding. If the patient wants a second opinion, be supportive. Be flexible, for life has thrown them a big curve. Most of all, just be present. Cancer is not contagious and they need you now more than ever.

If there is one takeaway we would like to impart from this book it's the fact that YOU can make a difference. YOU can help your loved one get through this awful treatment. YOU can donate blood and bone marrow to potentially save a life, and YOU can help to find the cure. You and I may not be the scientist that finds the actual cure for cancer, but we can help support those doing research and making the great strides in this battle.

Our prayers are with you and your loved one, and we wish for them strength and healing.

All our best,

Shannon & Erin

ABOUT THE AUTHOR

"The journey is the reward."

Shannon Benish is a financial advisor and mother of a brave pediatric cancer survivor. She lives in Dodge City, Kansas with her husband John, children Erin & Evan and step-daughter Sydney.

She enjoys attending her children's activities, doing home repair, reading, movies, travel, and watching football.

ABOUT OUR INSPIRATIONAL SURVIVOR

"The thing about being brave is it doesn't come with the absence of fear and hurt. Bravery is the ability to look fear and hurt in the face and say move aside, you are in the way."
~Melissa Tumino

Erin Pyle is an energetic high school freshman with aspirations of a medical career. She bravely beat cancer in February, 2014 and is now in remission. She enjoys movies, music, KU basketball, spending time with friends and family, and anything art related.

APPENDIX A

MAKING A DIFFERENCE

We wanted to share with you some of the organizations making an enormous impact in the lives of cancer patients today. One such organization is funding cutting edge research to find alternatives for individuals facing possible limb amputation. Several groups are focused on providing patient support and assistance in times of need. One is a facility we utilized during Erin's treatment that included an amazing group of oncologists and a nursing staff that always went above and beyond.

Please take a minute to discover more about the advances in technology, increases in patient quality of life and hope that is being offered to those fighting the battle.

For more information about each organization please visit our website at: www.howtohelpsomeonewithcancer.com

❖ Limb Preservation Foundation

❖ Rocky Mountain Pediatric Hematology Oncology and Rocky Mountain Hospital for Children

❖ Win the Battle Foundation

❖ Brave Hoods

❖ Roundup River Ranch

❖ There With Care

Made in the USA
Lexington, KY
14 March 2017